This book was brought to you by:

Reach Them To Teach Them is an educational outreach initiative from HustleUniversity.org. The methodology behind Reach Them To Teach Them combines: human psychology, individual learning styles, research-based data, pop culture and good ole' common sense to engage learners and energize the classroom making both teaching and learning a lively experience for both student AND teacher...everyday!

www.ReachThemtoTeachThem.com

BORED
OF
EDUCATION?

*Here are the REAL REASONS why
you NEED to go to School*

By Hotep

HUSTLE U INC.
New York   Atlanta   Los Angeles

BORED
OF
EDUCATION?

Here are the REAL REASONS why
you NEED to go to School

This book is dedicated to all teachers, parents, community leaders and youth service providers. We are all educators and charged with the task of improving the future. The fate of the world rests on our shoulders; continue to be strong!

To my parents, for being my first and best teachers.

To Mr. Slutsky, my first male teacher. Thank you for showing me that teachers can be fun and cool.

To Mrs. Good, my 6th grade teacher; the first one to show me the power of "tough love". You are who I patterned my own teaching style after.

To Dr. Alonzo Crim (R.I.P.), thank you for showing me how to be a "quiet storm". You were one of the greatest educators and child advocates ever!

To Mr. Maxwell, the first principal I served under. Thank you for giving me a chance and for teaching me how to be a professional.

To Dr. Strozier, thank you for being understanding and allowing me to "hustle while I work".

To my heroes, Marcus Garvey, Malcolm X, Muhammad Ali, Big Daddy Kane and KRS-1. Thanks for setting great examples for me to follow. Hopefully, I am doing the same for someone else.

To all the young people reading this, make sure you thank your teachers for caring enough to push you to be the best you can be.

Peace!

TABLE OF CONTENTS

A Note to the Teacher or Parent

FOREWORD:

In 2006, after teaching in Georgia's public schools for a decade, I began to realize that my students were getting better every year. Each new group I taught seemed to be better behaved and more fun than the previous one. I shared this sentiment with my colleagues at my school and quickly learned that they DID NOT agree.

I spent a few more years observing the children at my school and concluded that my co-workers were correct. The children I was teaching were not any smarter or more fun than the groups before. The children were not getting better, IT WAS **ME** WHO WAS GETTING BETTER!

Every year of teaching had given me an opportunity to try and measure different teaching techniques. I kept those that were effective and trashed those that didn't work. On my quest to become "the greatest educator in the world", I continually sought out more teaching techniques by attending conferences, reading books and observing other great educators at work and noting commonalities between them.

My quest also led me to encounter many educators and youth-service providers who were doing a poor job. Some knew that they were doing a bad job and simply didn't care. Most however, really DID want to help our troubled youth, but didn't know how.

To be honest, I didn't really think there was anything special about my teaching techniques. I took them for granted because they became second nature to me. In fact, because few of us actually get a chance to watch other teachers in action, I think we each assume that everybody else is pretty much teaching the same way.

I started realizing that I had something special to share in 2008 when I noticed that other educators at my school were consistently asking me questions about teaching techniques. Most of them were good teachers themselves; yet they saw something in me and my children that made them curious.

I call this thing....*The Light*.

The Light cannot be measured by standardized test scores and common analytical measurement tools used by public schools. The Light is something that resides in each of us, but for most, is very dull. The Light is spiritual in nature. It can only be witnessed by looking in people's eyes. The Light is made evident through people's actions, behavior and speech. Some call it a "vibe". At times, The Light shines so bright in people, it creates a visible aura.

The Light is the magic we witness in those rare moments when a student says, *"Aha! Now I get it!"*

Seeing this magical moment does NOT have to be a rare occasion. In fact, we can create this magic on a daily basis in our classrooms, schools, offices and homes.

In actuality, my fellow educators were not asking me about my teaching techniques so they could better teach Reading, Math, Social Studies and Science. They were seeing The Light in me and in my children and were inquiring to learn how they could brighten their own.

When a person develops this ability, it becomes a part of their very nature. (For one to be able to ignite the light in others, first theirs has to shine brightly.) This is why most people who know this approach seldom teach it. Like I had for many years, they assume it is common knowledge because it comes so natural and easy to them. They don't realize how special and unique their abilities are.

I was fortunate enough to have a life-changing experience that forever shaped the direction of my work.

THE EXPERIENCE

In 2007, I held a book signing at a local Atlanta mall. A teenager approached my table and I haven't been the same since.

This young man had long dreadlocks and a hood covering his head. He had gold teeth, dark skin, excessive gold chains around his neck and he wore his pants so low, he could barely walk straight. I wondered why he was coming towards me because he certainly didn't look like a reader.

Even still, I gave him one of my bookmarks. He read through the information that was on it and proceeded to look me square in the face and said, *"That's the realest stuff I ever heard! I need that."* He purchased a copy of my book (The Hustler's 10 Commandments) for himself and also bought a copy for his friend who was in the hallway behind him.

Needless to say, I was taken aback. First, I felt horrible for profiling the young man as a thug and non-reader. Second, because of what he SAID and third because of what he DID.

In those few words and small but selfless gesture, this young man had cause the The Light to go off in me. It was I who felt like saying, *"Aha! Now I understand!"*

It was this young man's response to a book I had written for adult entrepreneurs that helped my see something that rested right under my nose for many years. Not only did he help me see it, he made me realize its uniqueness and appreciate the need to share it.

Although he didn't say this, his words were like a heaven-sent letter addressed directly to me. This is how I interpreted the teen's response:

Dear Hotep,

You have written something that connects with me. This is something that I have been searching for, but could not find anywhere else. I want my light to shine. I need this; therefore I am willing to spend my own money on it. I know this will also help people like me who want to shine. I can help; so I will purchase one for my friend too. Thank You!

It was this single experience that led me to decide to share my approach to teaching with others.

THE APPROACH

I call my approach to teaching: **Education through Inspiration**

This approach cannot be *taught*, it can only be UNDERSTOOD. It comes from understanding basic truths about our humanity. Once these truths are understood, The Light will begin to shine in the educator. Consequently, the educator will begin to develop their own unique techniques for enabling The Light to shine in others. As the educator seeks further learning themselves, their techniques will become more refined and effective. This is what makes one a "Master Teacher"; not a degree, position or a series of letters placed after their name.

The following are the basic truths about people and education that all Master Teachers understand in one way or another:

The 1st Understanding- you have to be able to REACH them in order to TEACH them.

The 2nd Understanding- there is a big difference between EDUCATING and TEACHING.

The 3rd Understanding- students learn more FOR their teacher than FROM their teacher.

The 4th Understanding- people act in accordance to who they THINK they are.

The 5th Understanding- knowledge is NOT power; it is the ability to use knowledge that makes one powerful.

The 6th Understanding- children learn from what we DO, not from what we SAY. (Lead by Example).

The 7th Understanding- life is all about problem-solving.

The 8th Understanding- people teach us two things: 1) what to do and 2) what NOT to do.

A Letter to the Student

Dear Student,

Are you bored of education? Too bad!

To be honest, I didn't like school either! But I'm soooooo glad I had parents that made me go.

Unless you are one of the lucky few that have super teachers, school often feels like a mundane chore. GET USED TO IT!

There is no time in your life that you will NOT have to do mundane tasks; even if you are rich and famous.

Do you think it was fun for me to sit in front of a computer for months typing and editing the words that you are reading in this book? NO! It wasn't!

Do you think it was fun for **Michael Jordan** to practice free throws for hours everyday? No! It wasn't!

Do you think it was fun for **Bill Gates** to spend weeks writing codes to create his first computer programs? No! It wasn't!

Do you think it was fun for **Oprah Winfrey** to record a new episode of her T.V. show every day for 25 years? No! It wasn't!

Do you think it was fun for **President Barak Obama** to wake up early in the morning and travel to 3 different cities (in the same day) to speak to people about why they should vote for him? No! It wasn't!

But we did it anyway because all successful people understand that life requires a series of small, often boring tasks to be completed before we can enjoy the rewards. This is often called the fruits of our labor.

A problem many of you are having is that you are not seeing the fruits. There are way too many examples of people who have gone to school, worked hard and graduated but have not been able to be successful at achieving their real goals. Many of them are broke and miserable.

The other problem most of you are having is that you see the reward (the success), but don't know about the hard work that people had to put in to get it.

Sometimes it's hard to see how going to school has anything to do with being successful in the real world.

Well, read on!

Over the next few pages of this book, I'm going to show you exactly **how** and **why** school has everything to do with your success (or failure) in life. When you're done, you'll be soooooo glad you have the opportunity to go school…even when it's boring.

Sincerely,

Hotep

The Reasons Why You NEED to go to School

Reason #1: Practice The "Game Of Life"

Life is a game. If you learn how to play, you will "win". If you don't learn how to play well, you lose (hence the reason why unsuccessful people are called "losers"). School is the training ground for the game called life.

School provides a safe place for you to learn the rules of the game, practice and develop your skills. Yes, I said "safe place" because at school you are allowed to make mistakes without suffering the same dire consequences as you will in the real game.

If you fail in school you get an "F", when you fail in real life you go broke, become homeless, go to jail or lose your life!

So go to school! Try, try and try again. If you fail, press the "reset button" and do better the next semester.

Just like at the start of each video game, everyone begins the semester with a 100%. As you proceed, your task is to pass through the different levels (1st grade, 2nd grade....12th grade) and maintain as much of that 100% as possible. Each of these practice levels poses a more difficult challenge for you. Every time you successfully pass a level, you start the next with 100% again.

Like with any game, the more you play, the better you get; so make sure you seek higher education.

Go to college. Get a Masters degree. Get your
P.H.D.

Remember...practice makes perfect.

Reason #2: Learn To Solve Problems

Life is all about problem solving. In Math Class,
you will encounter word problems. Any teacher will
tell you that students have the most trouble with
word problems. Why? Because they have not
developed the ability to find effective solutions to
problems. This inability continues throughout their
lives and resurfaces later when they are adults as
a failure to solve real-life problems.

You see, all people have problems. The difference
between successful people and others is that
successful people know how to effectively SOLVE
their problems. Mathematical word problems help
you practice the process of finding solutions to
problems. The more you practice these types of
problems, the better you get at finding solutions.

You will learn that there is always more than one
way to solve any given problem. However, you will
also notice that some solutions will help you solve
a problem quicker and more effectively.

*Ex. Math word problems can often be solved by
counting, adding or by multiplying. Each process
will solve the problem correctly; but by multiplying,*

you will arrive at the answer a lot quicker (if you know your times tables).

Slow process: 1+1+1+1+1+1+1+1=8

Quicker process: 2+2+2+2=8

Fastest process: 2x4=8

You will see that some problems are alike. Therefore, you will become capable of solving similar problems by using the same strategy.

Ex. The key to solving many math word problems is to recognize clue words/ phrases that let you know how to solve them. Less than, difference, minus, and how much more, are all clues that indicate the proper way to solve a problem is by SUBTRACTING.

So go to school! Make sure you take great interest in word problems during math. Practice them often and you'll see how solving bigger problems becomes much easier too.

Reason #3: Scholars Make The Dollars.

I don't care how many times you hear the stories of wealthy celebrities or entrepreneurs who never finished high school; they only represent the lucky few. The fact still remains that scholars make the dollars!

In 1999, average annual earnings ranged from $18,900 for high school dropouts to $25,900 for high school graduates, $45,400 for college graduates and $99,300 for the holders of professional degrees (medical doctors, dentists, veterinarians and lawyers).

According to the Bureau of Labor Statistics the following were the 2010 annual salaries by education level:

Less than High School Diploma: $23,088
High School Diploma: $32,552
Bachelor's Degree: $53,976
Master's Degree: $66,144
Doctoral Degree: $80,600
Professional Degree: $83,720

90% of welfare recipients are high school dropouts.

According to a report from the U.S. Census Bureau, over an adult's working life, high school graduates can expect, on average, to earn $1.2 million; those with a bachelor's degree, $2.1 million; and people with a master's degree, $2.5 million. Persons with doctoral degrees earn an average of $3.4 million during their working life, while those with professional degrees do best at $4.4 million.

That means a college degree is worth almost twice as much in lifetime earnings than a high school diploma!

Why?

Because school is used as a way to separate the weak from the strong and the able from the incompetent.

Employers are constantly looking for ways to eliminate applicants from the selection process. The most common way to do this is to see if an applicant has shown the willingness to work hard at school. Employers feel more certain that if a person has worked through school, they will also "work" hard for their business. Conversely, a school "drop-out" looks like a quitter, and an employer simply doesn't want to take a chance on someone who has already proven to quit when the work becomes difficult.

Is it POSSIBLE for a person to drop out of high school and get a great paying job or start a successful business and become a wealthy millionaire? Yes.

Is it LIKELY? No!

So go to school, then go to college, then go to graduate school and continue on to get a doctorate or professional degree. Scholars make the dollars. The numbers don't lie.

Reason #4: School Strengthens Your Brain Muscles

School is the "gym" for your brain muscles.

Your brain is a muscle; and just like any other muscle in your body, it needs exercise in order to grow and become strong. You will find as you get older that people suffer from under-developed brain muscles. This happens when people spend too much time engaging in mind-dumbing activities instead of doing homework. What mind-dumbing activities? I'll tell you!

First is television. T.V. can be ok if you are watching the Discovery channel, the History channel, CNBC or any other education programming. Unfortunately, most people watch programs that have little or no educational value. Scientists have proven that most T.V. shows are non-stimulating to the brain and after 10 minutes of watching, cause brain activity to slow down. During this time, a person's brain waves match those of a person dreaming.

Yes, cartoons, Reality T.V., music videos, soap operas and talk shows literally put your brain to SLEEP!

Next is radio. Music stimulates our senses and emotions. More often than not, music causes interference to our brain waves and "drowns out" our thoughts. We enjoy music because of its ability to put us in a certain mood by taking us away from our own thoughts and replacing them with the thoughts of the singer.

Yes, music INTERFERES with your ability to think!

School however, actively engages your brain. It makes you think, ask questions, solve problems, debate and persuade. All of these activities provide exercise for your brain. Just like with any muscle, you want to exercise your brain often and make it challenging. The more work you do, the better for your brain. The more challenging work you do, the better for your brain. If the work is too easy, it doesn't help you learn anything and your brain won't grow stronger.

So stop being a wimp! Go to school and build those brain muscles or you'll get bullied as an adult by people who are smarter than you. They'll rip you off, force you to do things you don't want to do and you won't have any choice because you didn't finish school!

Reason #5: School Allows You To Have Options

The biggest difference between people who enjoy life and those that are miserable is the presence of options. Options give a person the ability to do whatever they please, whenever they feel like it. Having options is freedom. Not having options sucks!

Finishing school gives you options. The further you go, the more options will become available to you. Imagine a video game in which you are trapped in a maze filled with doors. Your objective is to get out of the maze so you can be free to do anything you want. Life is like this game. School provides you with the practice and the "keys" to go through the doors.

For every level of school that you successfully complete, you receive a key. Each key opens big, heavy doors that will allow you access to win freedom. Each key provides you with access to more doors. Without the keys, you will have to try to open these massive doors on your own. Chances are…that won't happen.

Here's why:

First, you can try to push the door open, but since your brain muscles are weak (because you didn't exercise them at school) the doors won't budge.

Next, you can attempt to pick the lock; but unfortunately for you, breaking and entering is illegal. So you'll end up in jail (like most people who don't finish school).

Lastly, you can ask someone to open the door for you, but they'll most likely say "NO" because they worked so hard for theirs, they won't think you deserve their help.

So go to school and collect as many keys (degrees) as you can. Once you do, nobody can ever take them away from you, so you will be free to walk, talk and dress however you feel.

"Do what you HAVE to do, so you can do what you WANT to do." – The Great Debaters (movie)

Reason #6: Learn To Read. Write. Speak.

There is 1 basic skill that is needed by ALL PEOPLE in order to be successful in life. That skill is called, Communication. If you develop the ability to communicate effectively, the world will be in your palms. The main forms of human communication are: Reading, Writing and Speaking. School is where you learn these precious and much overlooked skills.

Think about it! There are few jobs or businesses that don't require the need for a person to read, write and speak. Any job that doesn't require these skills is either very low paying, low-level or extremely dangerous. You certainly won't be a CEO or boss of anything if you can't read, write or speak well.

This is how it works:

1) You READ to acquire information. A person that has information is considered smart because they have knowledge. When a person is able to use their knowledge they become powerful and are able to do things other people can't.

2) You WRITE and SPEAK to demonstrate your power. When a person writes well or speaks with a command of the language people will believe what they are saying. People follow the words of those that are able to write and speak intelligently.

People who cannot read, write and speak well are less capable than their peers and end up following the written/ spoken words (directions) of others who can!

With this understanding, you would think EVERYONE would jump at the opportunity to go to school and learn these skills, right?

WRONG!

- *Forty-two million adult Americans can't read.*

- *Fifty million adult Americans are limited to a 4th or 5th grade reading level or can only recognize a few printed words.*

- *The number of illiterate adults is increasing by 2.25 million people each year.*

- *The number of illiterate adults includes nearly 1 million young people who drop out of school before graduation and 20% of all high school graduates.*

Since their job/ business opportunities become so limited, illiterate people are missing out on 237 BILLION dollars each year that they could be earning if they knew how to read, write and speak well.

The inability to read, write and speak well severely handicaps a person's opportunities to make a living. Therefore, many turn to crime or some other type of unwanted behavior. This is why 60 percent of America's prison inmates are illiterate and 85% of all juvenile offenders have reading problems.

The bottom line is: Go to school; and if you learn nothing else, learn how to READ, WRITE and SPEAK!

Sources: Education Portal (September 2007) and U.S. Department of Education

Reason #7: Learn To Deal With Crazy People, Dummies & Idiots

As a teacher, it hurts me to say this, but there are a lot of crazy people, dummies and idiots in school. Most of these students do not change when they get older. Well, actually they DO change; they become even more crazy, dumb and idiotic as adults! SO GET USED TO THEM NOW!

Part of the wide diversity we encounter at school gives us the "golden" opportunity to learn that some people just don't think logically:

- Some people haven't learned what most of us consider basic skills (like how to read, write or do simple math).

- Some people don't have what's known as "common sense".

- Some people will do anything (usually something bad, wild or dangerous) for attention.

- Some people are always angry and love to cause drama and mayhem.

- Some people have a warped sense of reality and make-up things that aren't true.

Well, I'm here to tell you, if you don't learn how to deal with them now, these people will end up driving YOU crazy later on in life!

One of the greatest challenges we all face is learning how to choose the right people in our lives. It has been said that a main reason why people fail is because of their inability to choose the right people. School is where you develop this ability!

- Students who haven't learned their basic skills need someone to help or mentor them. If they want to learn….help them. (You might become a great teacher or counselor one day.) BUT if they are the type of student that causes trouble in class or is a behavior problem because they don't know how to do the work, stay away from them.

- Students with no common sense are usually immature or inexperienced for their age range. Be patient with them.

- Students who crave attention are dangerous. There's no telling what they will do next. Stay away from them.

- Students who are angry and cause drama or other trouble are also dangerous. Stay away from them too.

- Students who have a warped sense of reality are hard to identify because you are often not sure if they are telling the truth or not. Some of them are very funny and entertaining. Only time and experience will help you deal with these people appropriately.

And that's exactly my point. School gives you the chance to have experiences with plenty of crazy, dumb and idiotic people in a controlled environment. So go to school and learn how to deal with them now; because unfortunately, you will be dealing with them in one way for the rest of your life!

Reason #8: To Learn Teamwork

Teamwork makes the dream work!

Working with a team is one of the quickest ways to become successful. School is the first place most of us have the chance to work with a team. Any group assignment is an opportunity for you to learn teamwork. Sometimes you have to work in pairs with a single partner, other times you are in groups of 3 or more. Even P.E. class gives you a chance to work in teams.

The power of working in teams is the capacity to combine your knowledge and abilities with that of others. This "collective knowledge" multiplies each team member's ability so that the team can accomplish more in a shorter amount of time. Working with a team also helps because you can learn from observing other people's methods of doing things and solving problems.

However, the REAL beauty about school is that it teaches us how to CHOOSE a team!

Teams are effective only when the right combination of people is formed. So YOU have to be able to identify people's strengths, weaknesses and different character traits in order to arrive at the right combination.

When you play football you need people to play different positions. You need a big person to block, a fast person to run, an accurate person to throw, and a tall person to catch.

Well, the same way you select people to form any athletic team, is the same process you use to form any team!

Ask any successful person and they will tell you the importance of having a good team, where people play their position. In my business (and most others) I recognize the need to have a team comprised of a person that: writes well, is a logical thinker, can do good research, is organized, speaks well and someone who is creative. Don't YOU need the same for any group assignment?

School is the place where you learn how to build a great team. You will learn how to combine different skill sets with others to get the best result. This is a skill that will be needed for the rest of your life (especially those of you who plan to run a company one day). Go to school!

Reason #9: All The Girls & Guys Are At School

This may seem obvious, but few people actually realize that school is where all the girls and guys are. Anyone who has been suspended or expelled knows this fact. THAT'S WHY THEY STILL COME UP TO THE SCHOOL AFTER THEY'VE BEEN KICKED OUT! School is the best place to make friends and socialize every day. Where else can you go to accomplish all of this in one single place?

School is the place that gives you an excuse to spend time with people you like.

- Schoolwork gives you a chance to sit next and work with a girl or guy that you think is cute.

- Homework gives you a chance to meet a girl or guy after school so you can complete the work together.

- Tests give you a chance to study together at open periods during the school day or after.

- Projects give you a chance to hook up on the weekends or during vacations.

For a shy guy like me, school was heaven! It was the ONLY place that I could safely talk to the cute girls without feeling too embarrassed. It gave me the opportunity to meet them and a "legitimate" excuse to talk to them. Those of you reading this that feel the same way, shout this with me..."THANK YOU SCHOOL"!

Reason #10: You Make REAL Friends At School

School is where you make REAL friends.

You might meet people on the various social networking websites online. Your page might even say that you have a few hundred (or a few thousand) "friends". But most of them aren't REAL relationships.

Real friendships can't be made online or by texting. Very few are established over the phone. Real friendships are made by spending physical time with each other. School is the place where you will have the majority of your face-to-face experiences with other people and therefore, make real friends.

School is also where many of your life-long friendships will be made. As an adult, chances are really high that you will one day: need help from, start a business with, date or even marry someone you once went to school with.

So get off the computer and your mobile phone and go to school! Meet lots of people and enjoy all the benefits of having REAL friendships.

Reason #11: The Future Leaders Are At School

Although there are a few exceptions, most of the world's wealthiest, most influential and important people have one thing in common...they all went to school!

Don't be stupid and try to be like that rapper, actor or athlete that is successful and dropped out of high school. Those people are the lucky minority. For each one of them, there are 10,000 more people that are homeless, broke or in jail who tried to take the same shortcut.

10,000 to 1 chances are not very good...don't bet on it!

The fact is, the future leaders of the world in every industry will have college degrees or higher. So if you are smart, you'll seek out higher education too so you can say, "I went to school with him/ her!"

You want to have high caliber friends; friends that have money and power; friends that can (and will) open doors for you. The best way for you to establish these kinds of relationships is by going to school with them. Study with them. Struggle with them. Share ideas and plans. Hold each other accountable. Eat lunch at the same table. Hang out together. This is how strong friendships are formed.

Then, when you are out in the real world and you need some assistance, it'll be so much easier to get the things you need. Why? Because all your friends own companies, run schools and hold political offices. They're doctors, lawyers and financial advisors, (and yes, some of them will be famous rappers, actors and athletes too!)

So go to school and make friends with all the nerds; chances are you'll either need or work for one of them in the future.

Reason #12: Build Your Work Ethic & Stamina

Success in any industry requires work. All the great religious holy books talk about the necessity of putting in work if you want to live. (The Bible even says that faith without work is pointless!) Sometimes, the work that needs to be done is repetitive and boring. Sometimes the work takes long hours. Sometimes the work is difficult. The people that are able to endure these moments and complete the work are the ones that are successful. And yes, you learn how to endure these moments in SCHOOL.

School helps you build your work ethic and stamina.

Remember the brain muscle and gym analogy I shared earlier? It comes into play again here. As you continue to exercise your brain at school, you become stronger mentally; your mind will be able to "carry more weight". This enables it to do more work....better, faster and for a longer duration of time.

School makes your mind strong. You can solve problems better and come up with more ideas when your mind is strong. Look around your classroom and observe those students who are able to solve word problems in math and explain their thought-process. They are mentally strong. Other demonstrations of mental strength are the ability to write a good essay or debate an issue with logical reasoning (reasons that make sense).

A strong mind completes work better and more effectively because it becomes used to doing certain tasks over and over. This practice causes the brain to find the best way to accomplish things and enables it to do things correctly, while using less power. This is called "muscle memory". It is the main difference between A and B students. An "A" student often makes schoolwork look easy, the same way the Incredible Hulk makes lifting a car look simple. School IS easy for the strong-minded because they can get good grades with less effort than others.

A strong mind will complete more tasks, faster. For example, some people can write out their times tables (1-12) in less than five minutes; while the same task will take others ten minutes.

Just like the athlete that can run up and down a field continuously without becoming exhausted, a strong-minded person can work for a longer period of time. This ability is called stamina. Standardized tests (those big, long tests you take at the end of the year) test your stamina. They make you sit quietly in a room for hours and read, read, read and write, write, write. All of that is designed to test how well you can maintain doing quality work over a given period of time. Yes, they use those tests to separate the strong from the weak!

People with a poor work ethic are lazy. They often complain about having to do work. Do most of your classmates complain about doing schoolwork? Of course they do! Because most students haven't developed a good work ethic! If they don't soon, they are setting themselves up for failure in school and failure in the real game too!

Don't be a loser! Go to school and build your work ethic. Do the class WORK and the home WORK. Trust me, it makes life a lot easier.

"School is work, so handle your BUSINESS!" – Hotep

Reason #13: Learn How To Deal With Supervisors

Since I ended the last section speaking about work, I'll continue in that context for this section.

I've heard students complain that they don't like or get along with their teacher. To these students I say...TOO BAD...GET USED TO IT!

All of us at some point in our lives will have to work under someone else's supervision. In the real game, we call them Managers or Bosses. Very few adults actually LIKE having a boss. Many adults don't even like their boss. (Ask your family members; they'll tell you).

Life is not always going to be fun. You will NOT like everything and everyone you encounter on your journey. The key to winning the game is learning how to deal with the things that you DON'T like.

Dealing with teachers helps us practice needed skills like: following directions, listening, accepting authority, obeying rules and being respectful. I know you probably hate hearing these terms, but you need to learn them. If you don't, you will find yourself dead or in jail!

I know you probably have plans of one day being your own boss and starting your own business or running an organization. That's great! But in order to get to that point, along the way you have to:

1)   Follow directions from people that know more than you.

2)   Accept that there are people who can take away your freedoms.

3)   Obey the rules of the environment that you are in.

4)   Be respectful to people in positions of power.

Don't be hard-headed and think you can succeed without these skills. You won't! Ask any wise, rich, powerful or successful person. Ask any person in jail that has learned their lesson. They will all tell you how necessary these skills are. Again, you don't have to LIKE supervision. Simply learn to deal with it!

School gives you this opportunity.

ALSO....

Throughout your school experience you will witness many different teacher supervision techniques. Some are more effective than others. Some styles you will like more than others. Pay attention! Learn from your teacher's example! Every teacher uses classroom management strategies to run their classroom. If you plan on being a boss one day, it would be wise of you observe these different strategies to see which ones you think you will want to use for your employees. But in order to observe the strategy, first you must endure the process. Go to school.

Reason #14: Learn How To Deal With People You DON'T Like

Like I said in a previous section, school is a great place to learn how to deal with things we DON'T like. One of those "things" is actually...people!

School provides us with a great amount of diversity. At any given time you can encounter different races, cultures, personalities, smart people, dummies, big people, little people, bullies, wimps, nerds, troublemakers, geeks, homosexuals, cool people, funny people, popular people, handicapped people etc. All of these people exist in the real world as well.

You need to be able to deal with all types of people. It's easy to deal with people that you like because it brings you pleasure; but what do you do when you encounter people that you DON'T like? School helps us answer this question.

If you don't learn how to deal properly with people you don't like your life will be similar to one of those stupid Reality TV shows where there's always some type of drama. These people are always fighting, gossiping, backstabbing, nagging and complaining; therefore, they can't focus on accomplishing their real goals in life.

You see people like this in school. They are always worried about what other people are doing or focused on bothering other students. These same people are doing poorly in school because they simply don't know how to get along with people they don't like. Instead of getting kicked off a TV show, though, these students get kicked out of school!

Learn what NOT to do from their poor example. Go to school, learn to get along with people you don't like and stay away from people that don't like you. Don't get caught up in the drama that losers create. Stay focused on your work and WIN!

* **QUICK HISTORICAL LESSON:** Adolph Hitler couldn't get along with people he didn't like and ended up destroying himself (and almost an entire country).

The lesson: Check yourself before you wreck yourself!

Reason #15: Learn To Set Goals & Achieve Them

School is the place where you will first learn how to set and achieve your goals.

Goal-setting is one of the most fundamentally important and equally overlooked skill needed for success. It sounds so simple, but unfortunately, many people do not set goals; and their lifestyle suffers because of it. Ask any accomplished person, and they will normally be able to describe their goals to you in detail. Ask the average person who is having a difficult life and they probably don't know what their goals are.

Setting goals is the first step towards achieving goals. If you aim for nothing, that's exactly what you'll get...NOTHING!

In school, you are taught (or should be taught) to set goals; then you spend the rest of your time working to achieve those goals. What goals do you have for yourself?

- *Do you want A's or B's?*
- *Is there an award you want to win?*
- *Is there a college you want to be accepted into?*
- *Is there a person you'd like to impress?*
- *Is there a group or team you'd like to join?*

Setting the goal is the first step towards achieving it. Once you know WHAT you want to accomplish, then you can focus your actions on the activities that are necessary to do it.

Sometimes you will miss the mark. Other times you will do better than expected; and yes, once in a while you will hit a bullseye. However, you don't want to be successful "once in a while". You want to be able to reach your goals ALL THE TIME. The key to being able to reach your goals consistently is in the practice that school provides.

Don't live your life accepting whatever comes your way. Have your own goals and expectations for yourself. Set high goals; you never know how far you can get if you don't attempt the journey.

So go to school. Set goals and learn what it takes to reach your goals. Practice, try, measure results, re-calculate, practice more, try again, score!

Reason #16: Practice Getting Up Early & Overcome Procrastination (Time Management)

School trains us to wake up early and helps us overcome procrastination.

Whether you like it or not, most business in our society occurs early in the day. What was once considered a "9 to 5" is realistically more like a "7 to 4". This means you will have to get up early on a daily basis if you want to take advantage of the many opportunities that are open during this time slot.

School is the place where we first learn the discipline of waking up early in the day.

Some people wake up early naturally; for many others (like myself), getting up early is a very agonizing task. If you are like me, you'll just have to get used to it. The key however, is in making the process easier for yourself. Here are some ways you can make getting up early less painful.

- Shower the night before.
- Have your clothes laid out the night before.

- Wear the school uniform, so you don't have to waste time figuring out what you are going to wear.
- Set your alarm clock 10-15 minutes ahead of the actual time.
- Eat a breakfast that you can carry with you.

School doesn't just teach you to get up early; it also helps us realize the value of ARRIVING early too. When you arrive to school early you can meet up with your classmates and finish an assignment that you should've completed the night before. If you arrive to class early you have to time to study or brush up on a needed skill for the day. Sometimes when you arrive early you can even get a "sneak-peek" at a lesson or test that your teacher is preparing. If you are early to lunch, you can select from the best food and choose the best seating area.

The advantages to being early are plentiful; and they don't just apply to school. As an adult, you will learn that the early bird gets the worm. There is a lot of competition vying for the same prize; if you are late, you will lose out to the person that was early.

The other time-oriented skill that school teaches us is to overcome PROCRASTINATION.

To procrastinate means to wait until the last minute to accomplish a task.

Many adults fail to achieve their dreams in life because they are procrastinators. They are given plenty of time to do something, but they wait until it is very close to the deadline to actually do it. Then, unexpected things happen which prevent them from meeting the deadline, so they miss it. This is why so many adults are late.

When an adult is late it costs them money. It's called a "late fee". So not only did they miss a deadline, but they lost money too. This is what happens when people procrastinate.

Since you are in school, you can see this same thing occur as well. You might wait until the day before the deadline to complete an assignment that you were given a week before. But, what if something unexpected happens like your Internet is disconnected? What if it is a Sunday and the library has already closed and you can't go to your friend's house?

The fact is, something unexpected ALWAYS happens.

So don't procrastinate. Go to school and learn how to best manage your time.

Reason #17: Practice Preparation

Whether its passing a test, scoring a goal or winning a contest…. everybody wants to succeed. But what many people neglect is making sure they are PREPARED for success when an opportunity presents itself.

"Success is where opportunity meets preparation."
– Hotep

The prize is often not awarded to the best, strongest or smartest....but to the one who is most prepared. I can't even count the number of dollars I've made not because I was smarter, faster, bigger or better-looking than the rest, but simply because I was better PREPARED!

People complain when they see someone who is obviously not the most talented person land a position or contract. You may have already had an experience when you felt cheated out of an opportunity that you believe you are more qualified for. Chances are...you are correct! You probably ARE more qualified and talented, but you probably weren't PREPARED for the opportunity when it presented itself.

School is where you develop and practice the necessary skill of preparation. Because you go everyday for at least 12 years, school gives you thousands of chances to be successful. Unfortunately, most students don't recognize the value of this opportunity. Many will fail, not because they are dumb or unable, but simply because they are unprepared.

Every class, every homework/ class assignment, every test, every question is an opportunity. They are opportunities to succeed. The students who properly PREPARE for each of these opportunities are the ones who excel.

YOU need to be one of these students!

Success doesn't happen overnight. Success occurs as a result of a person's habits. Preparation is a habit that is developed over time. There's no better time or place to learn the habit of preparation than SCHOOL!

So go to school. Carry your books EVERDAY. Come to class with pen/ pencil and notebooks (and bring extras). Use folders to keep loose paper neat and organized. STUDY for your tests. PRACTICE even when you have no homework. These are exactly the same things you will have to do as an adult in the real world.

Be prepared, or prepare to fail!

Reason #18: Test Your Mettle

Your mettle is a combination of your character, spirit and ability.

Do you really know yourself? Are you intelligent, fast, strong, attractive? How do you know? The truth is YOU DON'T; until you are able to compare your qualities with those of other people. School is the place where you are first able to measure yourself against others and really test your mettle.

See, we need to meet and socialize with other people. People provide a measuring stick for which we determine our own worth against. You may think you are funny now, but if you meet another student who makes people laugh even more than you, then you might realize that you are not as funny as you think.

Measuring our abilities against others is how we get a better perspective on ourselves. Then we can test our mettle through healthy competition.

- **Think you're smart?** Are you getting the best grades in the school?
- **Think you are athletic?** Are you winning 1st place?
- **Think you are popular?** Did you win the election?
- **Think you are big/ tall?** Is there a bigger or taller student in your school?

Have you tested your mettle yet?

You might be best in your class, but are you the best in the whole school, what about in the neighborhood, county, city, state, region, country, continent, world?

So go to school and see what you are REALLY made of. See how you measure up next to your peers. Every year you will encounter a new group, and therefore, a new challenge. There's nothing wrong with a little healthy competition. Just remember, you are not really competing with your classmates, you are competing with YOURSELF!

Prove yourself, to yourself.

Reason #19: Find Out What You Are Good At

School is one of the best places to find out what you are good at.

As a business consultant and success coach, I've learned that one of the biggest reasons why people have difficulty in life is because they don't know themselves. They have big dreams...but often fail at achieving them because they don't know their own skill set, strengths and weaknesses. School is where we learn these things about ourselves.

Take one look at your report card and you'll see what I mean. Your report often reflects your strengths and weaknesses.

- *A's reflect the things that come easy and natural to you.*
- *B's reflect things that you are good at.*
- *C's indicate things that you struggle with.*
- *D's and F's show that you are either: not trying, not paying attention, lazy or in the wrong class.*

If you are wise, you will start paying attention to these indicators. When you can identify your skill set and talents then you have a greater chance of being successful in the long run. This is how it works:

1) Go to school.

2)   Take as many different classes as you can (try them all).

3)   Try all the extracurricular activities available.

4)   Do your best all the time.

5)   After the class/ activity is done, reflect on whether or not you enjoyed the subject/ activity.

6)   Participate in more classes/ activities that you enjoy.

7)   Think about (and list) all the different careers or businesses you can start that utilize the skills you are developing in these classes/ activities that you enjoy.

8)   Research these careers and businesses you listed.

9)   Talk to people that are currently in these fields. Ask them to mentor you.

10)   Get jobs or intern in these fields.

11)   Go to college and major in these fields.

12)   Socialize and network with other people in these fields.

13)   Start your career or a business in these fields.

14) Seek higher education and always keep Growing.

15) Enjoy a fulfilling, exciting and happy life doing what you love!

What was step #1? *GO TO SCHOOL!*

Reason #20: It's FREE!

Name a place where you can play sports, meet people, learn money-making skills, develop music and singing ability, do arts and crafts and even EAT for free. That place, ladies and gents, is the American Public School!

Public school is probably the only place where you will be able to get so much opportunity for FREE! (Some of you will learn this the hard way when you want to go to college and can't afford it.)

It's sad how many people (young and old) complain about public schools. Most don't appreciate the fact that school is a free service provided by our government. What they don't realize is that school DOES NOT have to be free.

What if you had to PAY for elementary, middle or high school? Could your parents afford it?

Imagine if you were born in a country in Europe, South America, Asia or Africa where ALL schooling costs money! Most children in these countries actually WANT to go to school, but their familes can't afford an education. So the kids have to work all day instead of learn. Sometimes these families can only afford to send one child to school so the rest of their brothers and sisters wait home and hope their "educated" sibling can teach them what he/she learned that day. This is the reality for millions of people around the world. And some of us have the nerve to complain about something we get for free?

Shame on us!

The truth is, education is NOT FREE! It costs money; but YOU don't have to pay, other people pay the cost for you. Don't be arrogant and think things can't change. If people keep mistreating public school, the government might decide to get rid of it altogether.

So show you appreciate school. Take advantage of this free opportunity and make the most of it. You never know....if you don't use it, you might LOSE IT!

Reason #21: Avoid The "Trap"

If none of the previous reasons have convinced you that you NEED to go to school, this one should do the trick. Here are some statistics about the relationship between school and prison. The stats don't lie folks.

- *Research indicates that about 75 percent of America's state prison inmates, almost 59 percent of federal inmates, and 69 percent of jail inmates did not complete high school.*

- *Additionally, the number of prison inmates without a high school diploma has increased over time (Harlow, 2003).*

- *A ten percent increase in the male graduation rate would reduce murder and assault arrest rates by about 20 percent, motor vehicle theft by 13 percent, and arson by 8 percent. (Moretti, 2005)*

- *Of black males who graduated from high school and went on to attend some college, only 5 percent were incarcerated in 2000. (Raphael, 2004)*

- *Of white males who graduated from high school and went on to attend some college only 1 percent were incarcerated in 2000. (Raphael, 2004)*

- *State prison inmates without a high school diploma and those with a GED were more likely to be repeat offenders than those with a diploma. (Harlow, 2003)*

- *71.7 percent had less than GED Prep skills (less than 9.0 grade level). Admissions test*

*at around the sixth grade level; 71.7%
Below GED Prep Level*

It costs less to educate you than it does to incarcerate you. Yet, if you watch the news you will hear about the numbers of schools closing and teachers being laid-off. Meanwhile, somewhere close by, a jail is probably being overcrowded or a new one is being built.

There is a clear relationship between getting an education and going to jail. The facts above suggest that if you don't go to one, you WILL end up in the other. The choice is yours. As the song goes, *"You can get with this, or you can get with that"*.

AFTERWORD:

What more can I say?

I hope the reasons I've listed here were sufficient. If they weren't, then I challenge YOU to come up with your own list of reasons to go to school. Write your list down and remember it when things get rough.

I know school is not always fun and the work can be difficult; but so can life. I'm not trying to convince you to enjoy it, I'm telling you to GET USED TO IT!

It is NOT your teacher's job to make school fun. That is YOUR JOB! After all, it's YOUR EDUCATION!

Like most experiences, school is a journey. As you embark on the journey you will encounter challenges. Some will be easy; others will be very difficult to overcome. Your task is to find a way through. And if you can't *find* a way...MAKE A WAY!

Journey on!

Hotep

"SCHOOL IS YOUR JOB...HANDLE YOUR BUSINESS!"

PEACE,

ABOUT THE AUTHOR

Hotep (the Teacher's Teacher) is widely known for his unique approach to teaching leadership, entrepreneurship and social/ financial ethics by inspiring a love for learning and motivating youth to think critically and act responsibly. He is an Urban Education Specialist, and has developed a reputation for requesting the most troubled students and transforming them into willing participants in their own education.

Hotep has been using his unique methodology to reach learners and enhance performance for over a decade. He calls it "Education through Inspiration". He further assures that ANY educator can master this technique to reach ALL children from EVERY background.

EXPERIENCE FOR YOURSELF!

Hotep, "The Teacher's Teacher" preparing the next generation of educators.

www.ReachThemtoTeachThem.com

To Book Hotep for Speaking Contact:
404-294-7165
info@reachthemtoteachthem.com
www.ReachThemtoTeachThem.com

BOOK AVAILABLE:

"The greatest idea in the world won't work...unless you DO!"

Keep your day job and....

HUSTLE
While You
WORK

Using Your 9-5 To Jumpstart Your 5-9

HOTEP

www.HustleUniversity.org

BOOK AVAILABLE:

"Every successful person in the world owes their achievement in part to a woman. They are the backbone of all civilizations and the most powerful beings on earth!"
-Hotep, author of The Hustler's 10 Commandments

Ladies Are
HUSTLERS
Too!

A Collection of Corporate Best Practices, Ancient Wisdom and Guerilla Tactics for Today's Independent Woman

HOTEP
♀

www.HustleUniversity.org

BOOK AVAILABLE:

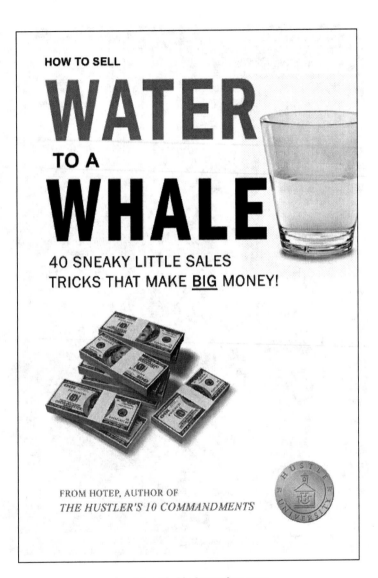

www.HustleUniversity.org

LEADERSHIP CURRICULUM AVAILABLE:

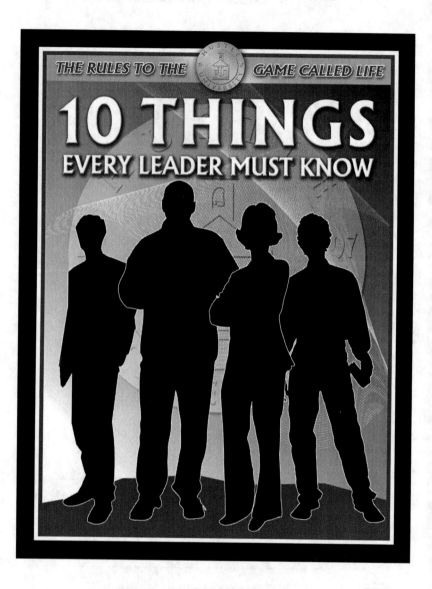

www.HustleUniversity.org

BOOK AVAILABLE:

www.HustleUniversity.org

ACTIVITY-COLORING BOOK AVAILABLE:

www.HustleUniversity.org

The Hustler's Guide
To The
Entertainment Industry

Limited Edition

R.A.B. PRESENTS A SKINNYMEN PRODUCTIONS FILM
"The Hustler's Guide To The Entertainment Industry"
CO-PRODUCED BY ERAJ MEDIA   MUSIC BY SKINNYMEN PRODUCTIONS
WRITTEN AND DIRECTED BY HOTEP   EDITED BY SKINNYMEN PRODUCTIONS

www.HustleUniversity.org

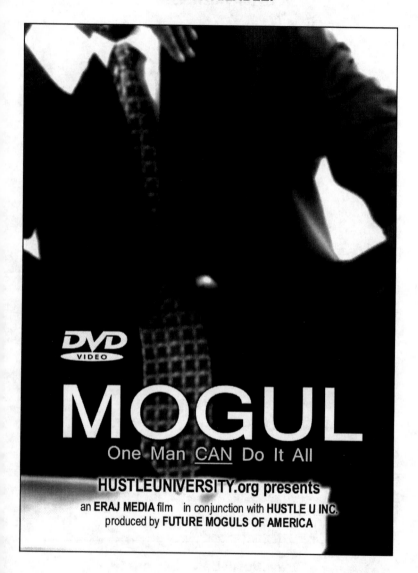

www.HustleUniversity.org

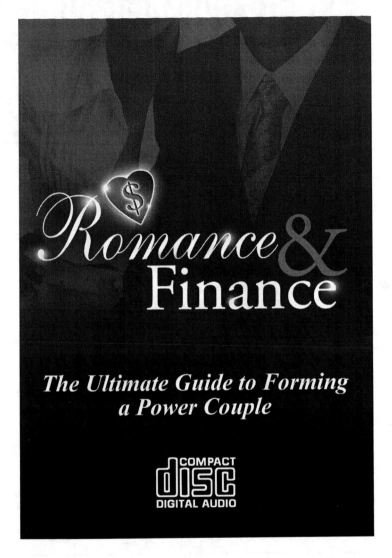